No Gods Are False

Augustine Bowe

DRAWING BY CLAES OLDENBURG
REPRODUCED BY PERMISSION OF THE ARTIST

NO GODS ARE FALSE

Selected Poems of Augustine Bowe

Selected and with an Introduction by
John Frederick Nims

New York : The Macmillan Company
London : Collier-Macmillan Limited

ACKNOWLEDGMENT

The following poems first appeared in POETRY:
*I Thought of These Things, It Took
So Long, It Minds Not, Rousseau in the Custom
House, The Fanciful Engravure of the Sky, Dies
Irae, The Queen, Change, Comet Near Vega,
Conquest of the Mind, The Crucifix, The Weight
of All This Air, There Must be Honesty in Kindness,
There Is No Explaining, The Strife,
The Frailty of Virtue, Numbers, Flux and Flow,
Between, The Worm Has Hope, Doubt.*

FIRST PRINTING

*The Macmillan Company, New York
Collier-Macmillan Canada Ltd., Toronto, Ontario
Printed in the United States of America*

Contents

CONTENTS

❧ Introduction

Augustine Bowe: A Memorial

(1893–1966)

He walked for miles along the lake every day, summer
and winter. And somehow it always seemed he was
striding into the wind. Or, when the season permitted,
even in his sixties he swam for miles along the shoreline.
More than once, as I watched him leave the water, his eye
alert, his gesture boyish, I had the sense that he had been
swimming against that current too, as he swam against so
many.

It is hard for me to recall his poetry without being
distracted by such images. For some years the Bowes'
lake-side apartment had been almost a second home; he had
been almost a second father. I felt free to drop in with
anyone, particularly with anyone who had literary interests:
with the girl from Bennington who ate all the fruit in
the centerpiece and became known as "The Banana Girl";
with the young playwright who could not quite afford
socks, but whose *The Glass Menagerie* was beginning to
catch the eye of the Chicago critics; with Allen Tate,
violin case under his arm, all ready for an evening
of Mozart duets with Julia Bowe, our hostess.

When we arrived it might be to find Oliver St. John
Gogarty, with his rollicking songs and his stories about
Yeats and the Irish Rebellion. Or we might find our host
in earnest conversation with J. Patrick Lannan, his close

friend of many years, about what might be done to save
Poetry, in times when Chicago's world-famous magazine
seemed in danger of going under forever. A subject for
Giorgione or Titian, these two friends leaning their
impressive—some would say "leonine"—heads together
across the crystal and the onyx, like Florentine princes
of the great days: Gus Bowe equally at home in the
courts of law and the libraries of literature; Pat Lannan,
with his spectacular collections of jade and modern
painting, equally at home in the worlds of power and
culture. Or, in a wild leap across the centuries from the
past of the Medici to the future of the "happenings" that
had not yet happened, we might find young Claes
Oldenburg, a friend of the Bowe children, quietly at
work on his drawing of their father.

Sometimes I would let myself in alone late at night,
and turn to the long living room that at first seemed empty.
The books all along one wall were in many languages:
my friend had been trained in Greek and Latin, and for
many years had spent every summer in France; his wife,
Julia, knew not only French, Spanish, and Italian, but
had studied Russian, Arabic—and even Hebrew so that
she might read the Old Testament in the original. Here
the ages met: above the ravine of books, the marble bust
of Dante scrutinized, from beneath the ceiling, Joan
Mitchell's brilliant canvas of the Tour de France. Entering
the dimly lighted room, I might not notice at first that he
was still up, in a favorite chair in his favorite corner,
reading perhaps, or writing, or pondering on the doubtful
doom of humankind, as the lap robe half fell from his
knees and the great draperies billowed around him in a
wind that blew not only from across the lake but from
out of time and space. Then he would be on his feet and

coming toward me—one of the few presences I have
known I would call noble—very tall, his brow
Yeatsian, his step springy even in old age.

We might have a midnight brandy and water, and he
might talk, with enthusiasm, but sharply, wryly, about
what he had been reading, about Surtees, perhaps, or
Toynbee, or Benavente. Or he might select one of the long
yellow pads at his feet, the lined legal tablets in which,
night after night, year after year, he wrote his poems. For
this was how he preferred to spend his evenings. The rest
of us might be out with the long-haired fruit-munching
cuties, who were doing term papers on subjects like "The
Authority Symbol in James Joyce," or we might be
pub-crawling with the visiting writers. He preferred
solitude to the society of all but a few; preferred poetry
itself to the company of poets.

The poems he read from these tablets sometimes hit us
with a not unpleasant tingle of surprise, like that of static
electricity. They were not quite what we expected,
these poems that opened with lines like:

> He is gone to smithereens,
> Drugged with dope and drink . . .

Or

> God said to Moses: "Ten commands
> Are enough for the likes of you . . ."

Or

> God, do not despair
> Of your experiment.
> There are apes more fair,
> More fit for merriment
> Twisting on their tails . . .

They seemed to us alive and jaunty, but we might wonder at first if perhaps they were too improvised, too slapdash, too high-handed with the demands of meter and even syntax.

Of course they reminded us of the work of Emily Dickinson, a favorite poet of his and one that he occasionally sounds like, though he was too independent to sound like anyone for very long. But she might have written his "Multitudes minimize the soul," and would surely have been proud of his "An oarlock can defeat the sea"—which even has her little trick of repeating a vowel sound two syllables later, as in "So drunken, reel her bees." Probably in *The Scallion and the Rose* he comes closest to her manner. He was certainly like her in indifference to publication and fame. He did have several poems in *Poetry* between 1941 and 1945, when it was edited by George Dillon, Marion Strobel, and Peter De Vries, but this was more an agreement with friends than submission to a magazine. After becoming president of the Modern Poetry Association, he refused to let the magazine have any more of his work, although he was encouraged by Karl Shapiro to contribute. Nor did he submit poems elsewhere. Instead, the yellow legal tablets accumulated over the years, as Emily Dickinson's little packets had accumulated, until finally there were hundreds. Occasionally selections or whole tablets would be handed over to a typist: five notebooks of 1938, for example, include what presumably he cared to preserve of his work up to that time. In preparing this selection of his poems, I have gone through more than fifty such typed notebooks and many of the handwritten originals: over fifteen hundred of the several thousand poems he probably wrote.

One saw at a glance that we were mistaken in thinking the poems mere improvisations. Many times the poet would rework the same piece again and again, laying it aside perhaps for years to return to it with a fresher eye and a stricter sense of poetry. Indeed, it is not always easy to know which of several versions should be considered the final one. It is clear that his apparent nonchalance was an air. Like Yeats, whom of all modern poets he admired the most, he seems to have taken great care to seem careless, taken great pains so that he might seem to have taken none.

Anyone who feels that the poems show too little concern for traditional technique would be taken aback, as I was, by his earliest work. With lines like "He is gone to smithereens" in our ears, what are we to think of stanzas like these, written before 1927?

> So if the cup be hollow,
>> Wine at the lips is red;
> Whatever sadness follow,
>> Let the forgetful dead
> Have, for their songs of grieving
> Looms to be ever weaving
> Joys for tomorrow's thieving,
>> When revelry has fled.

Or,

> Daylight is ever breaking upon some sleeping land,
> In thoughtless rhythm shaking white waves on
>> yellow sand.
> The woe that sleep has nourished, that sobbed
>> on night's dark breast
> Until its pain has perished when tears gave way to
>> rest . . .

Or,

> There stood a white-mailed figure all alone,
> Whiter than hawthorn branch he stood beside,
> And that was Tristram who had feasted not . . .
> She too was robed in white, and ghost to ghost
> The moon-mist drew her to the hawthorn tree . . .

Or,

> O you that long have travelled
>   The land of light and lies,
> Come now and see unravelled
>   The dark yarn of surmise.

These are very good imitations, or exercises in-the-manner-of. The first even has the stanza form of Swinburne's *The Garden of Proserpine*. The second is early Yeats, like the broken fourteeners of "I will arise and go now, and go to Innisfree." The third is Tennysonian. The fourth is pure Housman. There are probably even readers who would feel that these four pieces are more "poetic" than lines about going to smithereens. It is interesting to consider the difference for what it suggests about the nature of poetry. But perhaps even more interesting is the question of why a poet who could write so easily and mellifluously in several accepted manners should go on to the smithereen kind of thing at all.

No true poet is content to counterfeit the voice of another, no matter how well he does it. To write in someone else's manner is to be little more than a ventriloquist's dummy. The poet's bird has been the nightingale, or the skylark, or the raven—but not the mockingbird. What Augustine Bowe wanted to find was a voice of his own, a voice in which he could express his own experience of reality. And the reality of his twentieth century did not present itself to him in terms of weaving looms or yellow sands or ghosts in the moon-mist. He had something more urgent to say about the doubtful doom, and he needed his own voice to say it. I am more concerned here to present a friend for others' approval than to praise him myself, but I think it perfectly fair to say that my friend did indeed find a voice of his own. If I were shown a poem of his, one typically in his manner, I think I would recognize it as his even if I had not seen it before.

I cannot say that of all of his contemporaries. Perhaps one need not be as blunt as Yeats, who once surveyed a little group of eager-eyed poets and said something like: "Gentlemen, the one thing certain is we are too many." But still, contemporary poets—what plagues of them there are! A half hour spent in a bookstore specializing in literary magazines and "little" magazines and we can come up with the names of a hundred poets we are assured are promising. " 'New poets,' " wrote Jules Renard, "remember that term, for you will not hear from them again." Most of our hundred poets have no importance because they have no voice; they are the wax dummies of the Muse. Who remembers Alice Brown or Mary McNeil or Frederick Knowles or Josephine Daskam? Yet these were hailed in an important anthology called *The Younger American Poets*. It was published in 1904. And any anthology of "new" poets, of those who are the rage of a season or two, who give the readings and win the prizes, is full of the Browns and Daskams of the time—of the new poets who will never be old ones.

Augustine Bowe needed a voice of his own because what he had to say was his own. Skeptical, rugged, independent —he paid little respect to received ideas. Among his many notebooks are found a number of pungent apothegms:

"I said his head was empty—it is a pity it was not." "He talked almost always to himself, and it was a long time until he learned he was talking to a fool." There is the same sharpness in many of the poems, which, with a sense of cosmic mischief, turn upside down the ideas too many of us live by. Perhaps, he will say, faith can move mountains, but it might be better to leave the mountains where they are. False gods may do much good, he tells us; some prayers flatter God indecently; the first great error was arithmetic. Truth, he felt, is not to be imprisoned in the conventional phrases, since existence itself breaks from the categories. The apparently reckless technique of some of his poetry is explained by his own quatrain:

> Precision is the ultimate defeat;
>   Prosperous clouds are not precise of border;
> Mountains are not careful of their feet.
>   Imprisoned things are most obsessed with
>   order . . .

Precision in our contemplations is like thrift in our conduct—an insult to the nature of things:

> Thriftiness is the great vice
> Of women and men;
> They will have gold combed from them like lice
> Again and again.

For life proceeds by a kind of grand indifference to the trivia most of us live for. To express such convictions as these, he began by trying the voices of other poets, but found that none could speak for him.

In his mature work there is almost never heard the echo of another writer—perhaps most surprisingly, there are no overtones of Yeats. There might be a touch of

Wallace Stevens, another favorite, in just a few lines like
"The fanciful engravure of the sky." Or of Thomas
Hardy in certain combinations of the ironic and the
lyrical, in the jostling together of the jaunty and the
gauche. One does not look for unity of tone here; the poet
himself would have disdained a uniformity he would
have thought false to the welter of experience. The strong
sense of incongruity he felt in the universe expressed
itself in ironic juxtapositions. Among cypresses and monks
and the lazy dapple of orchards we are brought up short
by coming upon ham-hocks and garlic and barges of lard;
at the solemnities of a funeral, our attention is called
to the feedbag of oats that keeps the undertaker's
horse glossy. Though the poet could write a traditional
lyric legato in lines like

> My lady, winds are blowing
> You have not heard before . . .

he often deliberately twitted the rhythm into contortions,
as if making fun of the punctilio of meter. With the most
serious subjects, he is likely to be most flippant. To
express the inscrutability of God in creation he uses an
image grotesque as any in the poetry of Edward Taylor:

> That one was bright:
> Left no tail-light showing
> In the night.

An image that seems almost mischievously meant to
perplex the reader: how is one to take *that*, the image
of God as a car disappearing around a corner, or as a giant
mechanized firefly? In these sudden outbursts of rowdiness,
of what Hopkins called "tykishness," in these abrupt
angularities, these frank unprettinesses, the poems at times

remind us of Romanesque or Gothic: the impish tricks of rhythm and diction are like the goggling faces that peer out of the capitals of St. Trophime, or like the leering gargoyles of Notre Dame. This is mockery that mocks even itself.

But the cloister is not only its freakish column, nor the cathedral only its gaggle of gargoyles. Though conscious of incongruity and able to jest about it—what Irishman is not?—Augustine Bowe had a deeply serious mind, deeply committed (as we say now), committed not only to issues of the day but also, but especially, to the mystery of our existence. Although I would hardly call him a Tennysonian poet, in thinking of him and his work my mind comes back again and again to "the doubtful doom of humankind." This seems to have been what he contemplated day and night, and accounts for a remote Celtic melancholy, a sense that his mind was off with the old unhappy far-off things in what should have been his most festive moments. Time and again I have watched his thought drift away from the "perfect" martinis by the lake at sunset, or from the bloom of wine and candlelight a little later, or from the vivacity of the evening's talk and music—for the company, if he had company at all, was exciting—have seen it drift away and knew it was with Julia, the wife he loved so much ("I found a face in all the million faces"), or with his son John, young and endangered in a world at war, or with his pretty daughter Julie Anne, about to have a child, though she herself had survived childhood only with the risks of insulin. Or it might be with all of us, or with the doubtful doom itself: the great face of death, which, although he lived to be a vigorous seventy-three, was daily as present to him as to any monk of Zurbarán.

xvi

"Be mannerly with death," he counseled us. He was always mannerly himself, and death returned the courtesy. He had been striding along the lake as usual, one cold February day—when suddenly, in an instant, he was not striding there at all, but in some other dimension: off into the winter clouds, we might imagine, or into one of the inscrutable regions he had speculated upon all of his life. As people gathered, death too was tykish and had his joke: the walker had not bothered to carry wallet or identification, and it was hours before anyone knew that the tall figure in the snowbank had been the Chief Justice of the Municipal Court of Chicago, and among the most distinguished of the city's million faces.

JOHN FREDERICK NIMS

No Gods Are False

⟨ I Thought of These Things

Cypresses in the afternoon,
Monks at plain-song in the chapel,
And the four phases of the moon,
Orchards and their lazy dapple.

I thought of these things, you have too.
How maidens have been moved by song,
But something strange and bad and new
Kept me from sleeping all night long.

Kings in their smoldering palaces,
The embolisms of the strong,
Wine that did not change in chalices,
The eloquent righteousness of wrong.

1

❧ *Winds Are Blowing*

My lady, winds are blowing
You have not heard before,
And there are oarsmen rowing—
What God do you adore?
The latchet that's undoing,
You shuddered at it once,
But here comes God a-wooing
Punctual as a dunce.
Lady, walk slow and humble,
Not fleetfoot as before.
There is a frightful stumble
Just outside your door.

The Face of Water

Pale is the face of water
    That only knows the skies,
Pale as a blue-eyed daughter
    That takes her mother's eyes.

But willows overarching
    Give mystery to streams,
And leagues of high cliffs marching
    Fill the deep sea with dreams.

3

Meant to Grow

Things were not meant to grow in line or furrow:
  Tumultuous generation moves.
Nowhere in nature may life burrow
  In neatly planted grooves.

To till a field with plow is to offend
  The natural laws of growth.
Thrift and labor ill can tend
  The heritage of sloth.

With cage and furrowed field we seek
  To teach life cautious ways,
Imprison grain to serve the meek,
  Keep thought within a phrase.

It Took So Long

Let us all believe,
Quiet our fearful hearts,
Wrap rosaries round the sleeve
Of him that parts.

Let us in prayer
Annul the doubting thought
That barricades the stair
Legend has wrought.

Let us all believe
In our eternal glory.
It took so long to weave
A hope so hoary.

It Minds Not

When joy points to a star,
Or needs the full of moon,
Then it has gone too far,
Will leave too soon.

But when beside the grate,
Or an enameled stove,
It minds not star or fate,
Then it is love.

Rousseau in the Custom House

No leaf within the jungle growing
Had quite the green he gave to leaves,
No leopard had a flank so flowing,
As his unseeing eye retrieves.

Letters stenciled on strange bales,
The smell of dried-out tropic things,
Invade his soul; his brush impales
The emerald look of unseen wings.

The Fanciful Engravure of the Sky

The fanciful engravure of the sky
Engenders much inebriate thought.
The pig may from his muddy sty
See all the wonder night has wrought,

But that does not distract him from the trough.
A pail of swill has more immediate meaning
Than stars that on mysterious errand wander off,
Where snout can never snuffle at their gleaning.

ᗷ Doubt

Faith can move mountains.
Let the mountains be.
For when mountains stir
There is no peace, even in the sea.

Doubt dares not touch
The heft of stone,
For fear it's better, much
Better to leave things alone.

More Frugally

The universe, inanimate,
More frugally than man
Keeps every hue and every sound,
And winds them on old spools around,
So somewhere in her attic rests
A memory of all her guests.

The Scallion and the Rose

Scallions are more prompt of growth
Than roses dare to be.
Fragrance has a way of sloth
That suits not husbandry.

But when the scallion blows his breath,
You will not thank its haste.
When you have smelled the rose in death,
You will not blame its waste.

No Way of Knowing

The sky has so little guile,
Men watching with care
After a little while
Can chart and compare,
Compute and compile
What storms she will dare.

The stars have so little skill,
They leave a great track;
Comets will
Come wandering back,
Like sheep one might kill
On a slaughter-house rack.

Who set the whole thing going?
Walked out of sight?
There's no way of knowing.
That one was bright:
Left no tail-light showing
In the night.

Applause

The sheen of diamond may be imitated
 Sufficient for the glances of the crowd,
And none but those that are initiated
 Will know a note is false if it be loud.

The measurement of dram and millimeter
 Was not devised so ham-hocks should be weighed.
Fame finds so many noises to defeat her
 She wants applause by centuries delayed.

The Answers

I must know all the answers.
It will not do for me
To dish up tunes for dancers,
Tweedle-dum and dee.

If I rig out a rhyming thought
That half explains your woe,
No melody however wrought
Need speak of where you go.

But that is what you ask of me.
Like Delphi's steaming earth
I must invent a blasphemy
That will explain your birth.

 *Between*

Neither beginning nor end counts so much
So much lies between
The eye, the hand will such things touch
Before the end of green

That Gods upon their stony hills,
Infants stirring in the womb
Tolerate the involved quadrilles
Whose last step is the tomb.

An hour or season will be soft,
There will be talk and song.
We can hold such flags aloft
Dark and silence will seem wrong.

The worm has hope
That fattens in a skull,
Smooths his snaky rope
Some irony to mull,
Some irony that saw
Stars helpless in the sky
And laughed at the stern law
That dragged them nightly by.

 *Plaster*

It was a bit of Staffordshire
Grandmother bought for homely cheer
That stands surviving, smiling here,
And with indifferent joy forgives
The hope that tired no longer lives.

The skirt is lifted with such grace,
Enamelled so the pleasant face,
And the red plaster of the rose
Is fragrant to the plaster nose.

Raised upon the window sill
The silly slipper waits until
A feather-duster will embrace
Some tangle of its plaster lace.

Poor old lady, what if she
Did this ruined beauty see?
At some plaster heaven's gate,
Plaster deities await.

A Whisper

I choose to improvise,
The chapel is lonely.
One may be wise
Where many are only
An uncomfortable crowd.
A whisper may be too loud.

Lucky to Knock About

He had not expected them to argue so
Over the mystery of the Trinity.
He was inclined to say, "Let it go! let it go!"
After all, divinity is divinity.

Why should we ponder on how God disposes
His own powers in His triune self?
We are lucky to knock about, smell garlic and roses;
We need not rummage his upper shelf.

He should not have tried to explain;
Should have remained distant and discreet;
Let his grace mysterious as rain
Fall and glisten on the street.

We argue like servants understairs
Over who sits at the master's table.
A servant has decent livery that he wears:
His master is well served and comfortable.

Dies Irae

Black velvet hangs on the cathedral walls.
The organ, death-struck, is wailing.
They read the office in the sanctuary stalls,
The beggars kneel at the iron paling.
The hearse must be back in town by three.
There is an hour for death, an hour for tea.
Hostlers must curry the mournful mare;
Oats do better than graveyard air
To polish her black and glossy sadness—
Than all this plush Gregorian madness.

❦ The Queen

The peacock looked at the queen's blue velvet
As it spread so softly down her thighs.
And the jewels at her throat, he saw them too,
And he saw the proudness that was in her eyes.

The thrushes listened to the queen singing
And were abashed when she stroked her golden harp
And the water grew a film that reflected
Her and hid the ugly spines of carp.

The Ambassador walked on the grassy lawn
Near the queen surrounded by her court.
Said: All of them that looked upon
Her have brought us but a pale report.

The queen looked on the peacock in wonder,
She heard the thrushes and her harp was still.
The beard of the ambassador she stood under
Seemed like a storm cloud on a nearby hill.

Change

For a little, ever so little while
Winds will be still, lawns will be green,
Fat sheep will stumble over the stile,
The lazy dial on his shadow lean.
Then will come dark days of change,
When shadows can confuse the hour,
And winds will wander cold and strange,
Venture and try their frosty power.
Plainly a careful man can see
The sun on tiptoe flee the north,
But why does he lose heart and flee,
And not as brave at dawn come forth?
Someone must yet deface the dark,
Upbraid the lazy lingering dawn.
The priest has gone, but left his clerk,
And I am that unhappy one.

Comet Near Vega

You are lost in the excitement of Christmas and the war.
Somewhere in the misty northwest sky,
For some reason, I forgot what for,
This December you are hurrying by.
In June and peace, strong glasses would be out,
And children would be standing on the hill.
Astrologers have much to say about
Your wayward fire, but you must wait until
Wars are afoot and Christmas is at hand,
And the world is filled with the Bethlehem star,
And the whole sky is blasted on the land.
Things are wonderful enough as they are.

Conquest of the Mind

How did I rise with all this armor on?
Who put this halberd in my hand?
How is it all the enemy are gone,
And I am sovereign of this land?

Here is a stretch that Caesar once disputed,
Here Horace was, his Sabine farm;
The chains of Euclid once this land computed—
What amulet had they, what charm?

The pride of an alderman may get a bloody nose,
Conqueror be sledged down like a sullen ox,
But here are colors to relight the rose,
And folk that have survived the pox.

The Crucifix

They came. Well, yes, they came,
As I had always thought they would,
But over and over they said the same
Words, because they thought they should,
To me nailed here in public shame.

Have you ever tried to hold the attention of a child?
Being God is something like that, if you take it seriously.
The guilty ones are too meek and mild,
The earnest ones behave deliriously.
I wanted them to be gently wild.

Perhaps the priests are right to give them beads
To tell, invent monotonous response
To endless litanies. They know their needs.
If they came unrehearsed and saw me all at once,
They would run madly off among the weeds.

The Weight of All This Air

The weight of all this air is such,
Spaded earth will not increase
The burdens that I carry much.
I will wear it like a fleece
To save me from a raw cold day.
It will cover up my eyes,
Stop my ears from what men say.
I will fancy I am wise.
I will nourish, sip by sip,
The earth that nourished me,
And I will hear from her own lip
I am from bondage free.

There Must Be Honesty in Kindness

There must be honesty in kindness;
It must look beyond a bowl of soup, a night of rest.
It must not be a momentary blindness,
An obstinate refusal to see the sunset in the west.

A fortnight in the country is a good thing for a child
But there are more than a score of fortnights in a year,
And some of them come when the winter is wild.
The youngest infant will grow old and full of fear.

We must hold many a hand that is dying,
We must feed many a face many winters through;
And many an angel on white wings flying
Has less to do than we have to do.

Of Crumbled Column

Now that of crumbled column
We make a smaller chapel,
Of gods too grave and solemn,
Rosaries that dapple
With little pills of prayer
The never-ending air—

Images once mysterious
Of gods that late there dwelt,
Stripped of their forms, imperious,
Let their wounds be felt.
And gods and men now mourn together,
Forgetful they might be masters of the weather.

His Hands Alive

Mozart may still assemble
Four violins, four men
That Mozart's hands dissemble.
Tell me, what is death then—
Could he, his hands alive,
His hands alive, more shake them?
There is no need for five;
We do not need to wake them.

Headdresses

We build dogmas over our brains,
Savage headdresses of paint and feather;
Assuage perplexity and pain,
Converse devoutly with the weather.

❧ *Errors*

So many errors of calculation,
False logarithms, comets astray.
God is ashamed of his own aberrations,
Humiliated when we pray.

No Gods Are False

A false god may raise up a true man;
With stony nod, soft virtues scan;
And prophets that foretell false things
May touch the sweetest of harp-strings.

No gods are false, they are all true
That tribes, for peace and mercy, sue.
In brazen calf, Buddha, we find
Some elements He left behind.

But There Are Nights

Mother of God, there still is pain,
Still is regret, there still is longing,
The sad, soft bitterness of rain,
The faces of those we have been wronging.

Mother of God, you and your child
Have only simple and deep emotions,
But there are nights when winds run wild,
And tumult disconcerts the oceans.

33

Meaningless Precision

Amoebae divide and divide,
Perpetuating the lowest form of life
What is there to admire beside
The meaningless precision of the knife?

Grief

Your grief is the great thing about you.
Other creatures do better with flesh and fur;
A gangling sunflower will surmont you—
But winds have an uneasy stir

When you decide on grief;
Stars shudder to their bones,
In sultry air the leaf
Dangles, and the reed moans.

More Fierce Than Love

There is no more stern grasp than this:
A man seized in convulsion.
There is tiring of caress and kiss,
But no sign here of revulsion.
The automatic action of
The entrails is more fierce than love.

The artery that is tired,
The heart's regurgitation,
Like batteries cross-wired,
Defy all cogitation.
Half a dozen galvanic gestures
Divest the soul of its earthy vestures.

True Hunger

If sweet is all you want
Things stay much as they are:
Petals the bees haunt
Keep the shape of star.

But if your hunger's true,
Tooth and fang will bite;
Have bones to grind and chew
In the dark cold night.

❧ *Experiment*

God, do not despair
Of your experiment.
There are apes more fair,
More fit for merriment

Twisting on their tails—
Be done with us.
Think of the patient flails:
What noise, what fuss

It is to get a grain
Free of its chaff.
Be cheerful, try again.
Do not frown. Laugh!

The Lake, the Star

The little lake filled all its shore,
Nibbled an overhanging tree;
Did not suspect there need be more
Expanse of water in a sea.

The gorgeous star that tossed upon
The ample billows of the night,
Thought not of being lost upon
The little acreage of sight.

Sabbath

This day is not for toil.
Rest arm and thigh.
This day, till not the soil,
Let bird go by.

Let loom and hearth be still
One day out of seven,
The stream flow by the mill
Reflecting heaven.

Incongruity

Little men move the great machinery,
Cranes and derricks from place to place.
Blunt shoulders push Wagnerian scenery;
Sleepy lenses comets chase.
The earth is filled with incongruity;
Cats are always laughing at queens.
Lineage of kings lacks continuity;
The lofty campanile leans.

Magdalen

She loved everyone she saw,
And many that she did not.
God need not have made it law,
Contrived an ecclesiastical plot:

She loved Him in spite of His artifices;
She listened to His beatitudes.
She covered His feet with kisses
As though His words were not platitudes.

Infinitely rippled was her falling hair,
As black and rippling as her fallen virtue.
Her avowals might be soft, easy to tear,
But her soft heart did not know how to hurt you.

Another Story

Poisonously pious was his prayer;
He flattered God indecently.
The drabbest raiment did he wear
And was never bathed recently.

He stood by the ticket dispenser
To sneak in and out of Purgatory,
But God smelled him over the smoke of the censer
And what happened is another story.

Let's Say "Good Night"

So far, not bad. Let's say "Good night."
A quarter of the moon is showing.
Stars walking brisk and bright,
A warm wind blowing.

But when light comes to end,
Moonlight faded, there am I
With only dark fields to defend
Under a coal-black sky.

The Dead

Dead men keep their fingers on a trigger;
Dead men have weapons they can use.
Targets grow bigger and bigger,
Truce of all sort refuse.
If you keep listening to voices of the dead,
There will be no peace ever anywhere.
The sun will rise angry and red;
Night will be a dark and sullen stare.

Mes Pensées, M. Perrichon

1

It is time now
I should have something to say.
I have been on the earth fifty years;
It is time I had seen things worth telling.
And if I have not,
That too is worthy of mention.

2

Beware the man that believes.
Distrust the man that doubts.
But the man who believes while he doubts
Is apt to be a useful friend.

3

Avoid the man that looks always at the grave.
Beware the one who never looks that way.
A heavy stone weighs too much on the mind—
Only a fool thinks stones are made to sit upon.

⁂ Roundsmen in the Night

I envy no man for his beer;
I wish no man's wife.
And yet I know my staying here
Will not be furthered but by strife.
There must be musketry at call;
There must be roundsmen in the night.
There must be lock and bolt and all
The shuddering armory of fright,
So that we sleep this night in peace
And wash our waking eyes with dawn.
Only mutton (broth and fleece!)
Trust, and nibble at the lawn.

The Old Gentleman

The cornfield runs down almost to the river.
He kept a road where his bay horse could run,
A bright clay pathway, narrow as a sliver.
Now sputtering lumbering trucks that weigh ten ton
Go shunting down the pathway of his pattern.
No tawny mare, no hackney coach goes past.
His heirs have all gone slovenly and slattern;
The brightest fancy has not long to last.

Sargent said a portrait was a painting
With something wrong about the mouth,
But nature never tires of acquainting
Us with faces out of plumb, north and south.
There are more lovely souls than lovely noses,
More beautiful thoughts than coral lips.
That is why thought is not imposed on roses,
And silk is put aside before it rips.

Gone

He is gone to smithereens,
Drugged with dope and drink.
Gone with lecherous kings and queens,
Quicker than a wink.

Gin can do a sovereign in;
Whiskey can make a foolish saint.
Skies sober men expect to win
Are cozy, neat and quaint.

The heaven that a brawler sees
With his alcoholic eyes
So dazzles, his unsteady knees
Refuse to kneel before such lies.

The Dragon

You did not look at what you feared.
You hurried so in stumbling flight,
Fled faster as your gatepost neared.
You made a nightmare out of night
That darkened but to be endeared.

There Is No Explaining

You have memories we do not share,
Preoccupied with a nervous care,
Pulling vestiges of your soul
Out of customs, paying toll.
I do not know where you are going—
Do not look for any help from me,
Where smoky tugs are towing,
Once they untangle from the quay,
The wreckage of your seventy years;
There is no explaining this with tears.
You are right to be worried;
I would be worried too.
Right not to be hurried;
I would not know what to do.
I would breathe hard, wrap my flesh around its bone,
Shudder going out on the dark water all alone.

The Strife

This sense, that bereft,
The heart beats on in faith,
This nerve deadened, cleft,
Throbbing, thoughtless lather;
Ventricle freshening blood,
Blood mending tissue worn,
Till the dark nervous flood
Dykes of the brain have torn.
Tired of cobbled prance,
Living takes to cloud,
Heart alters its dance
So flesh is half a shroud,
A strange outpost of life,
Whose gospel is not writ:
This intravenous strife,
Death pulling at the bit.

The Frailty of Virtue

The seven deadly sins stood up.
The cardinal virtues were still on their benches,
Gluttony and Envy quickly sup,
Lust dragged Sloth and the rest of them off after wenches.
The cardinal virtues had so gently dined,
Only one had wit enough to say, "Shall we visit the sick?"
One shuddered at the way Covetousness and Lust en-
    twined,
He had not strength enough to pinch the wick.
"We have been outvoted," said Humility,
"By the seven deadly sins.
There are only four of us, and our scones and tea,
And there are seven of them now carousing at the inns."

Genetics

Rough hands are laid on amorous horses;
Hounds must love the proper hounds.
Cattle are bred so no remorses
Assail the ones we keep in bounds.
Only our peasants breed at random,
Have here and there a pensive child
That shudders when we shove and command him.
The rest are amenable and mild.

Argument

This and that way did you talk.
At last I was not sure
Your step was firm enough to walk,
But argument must endure

More flinty scarps than we can see
And hills where no grass grows.
What you say convinces me.
But why these upturned toes?

The Cold Face

Now and again we have a jolly dinner,
Now and again a jovial afternoon.
You can pretend to be a lusty sinner,
But not to the cold face of the frozen moon.

The Best It Could

What could be said upon this page
Should stop my hand from persiflage.
Who would twit the setting sun
For things that daylight left undone?
Summer did the best it could.
Remember all the trees were wood.

Numbers

The first great error was arithmetic;
There have been many since, but that was the first, the
      greatest
Flame that lit the wicked wick,
The pathway to the latest.

If, for instance, a million men
Were beyond all ways of counting,
If numbers stopped, as in a sense they do, at ten,
Mountains of horror would not keep on mounting.

One man can do a vast of harm,
But when you teach him sums
He will assail not arm to arm,
But with his inky thumbs.

❧ A. M. D. G.

You did well by the fifty-cent chicken dinner;
Some crumbs and some gravy are spilled on your vest.
Try the paddle-wheel now; you may be a winner.
He died when the sun was three hours to the west.

It is twenty-five minutes after two.
A soldier was lifting a sour wet sponge;
In pity he gave his spear a lunge
That pierced his side—it seemed the decent thing to do.

A fat old woman with a cheerful face
Has been grinding green cabbage all afternoon,
Grinding it into edible lace.
Out near the graveyard is a hurdy-gurdy tune.

God made them all: he gave them loaves and fishes,
These unwholesomely lean, these fat unwieldy people.
He must have known about these paper dishes,
And the asbestos roof they want to buy for his steeple.

A Song

He was young,
Young, as I was,
Soft of lung,
His beard soft fuzz.
I loved him and you know
I had a child before he let me go.
Not long and he was fat and old,
His child was stupid and cross.
Like a fool I tried to hold—
Then to my sorrow and my loss,
Child and father left me flat.

Can you make a song of that?

Village Idiot

My wits are not geared to
The wits of other men.
Somehow I am endeared to
Swamp and bog and fen.

Words walk lame and crazy
Over my luckless tongue;
Wishes spring strange and hazy;
Wild brass bells are rung.

The town has decent learning.
My wit must bestride
A strange uncertain yearning
I cannot learn to ride.

꧁ Ragged Bones

I walk the cemetery through.
Bones are more or less free under grass;
I feel them in the chilly dew—
Naked distals tingle as I pass.

Thank God for stones that keep them down!
Ragged bones half free of flesh would rise
On half a thigh, come galloping to town.
You're never sure what part of a man dies.

Have you ever seen a ghost?
Dead men are walking through my brain.
A ragged rock upon a seething coast,
I beat back death, again, again.

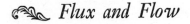 *Flux and Flow*

Let cottagers' children share the school,
Have dancing and all of that.
Just as much chance to play the fool
As the child of a high crowned hat.

Mill hands must have a turn at Latin,
Chimney sweeps a spot of Greek,
Soot should find its way to satin,
Soft-raised maidens learn to speak

To lanky lovers from the mill.
The world should be all flux and flow.
And the high house on the hill
Should have no means of saying no.

☙ *Ten Commandments*

God said to Moses: "Ten commands
Are enough for the likes of you.
Logarithms make such demands
For the curves of a drop of dew,
For parabolas of a breeze,
For the chemistry of trees.
Ten commands are enough," God said,
"For the likes of you to abide.
Tend the sick and bury the dead.
I must go now and arrange the tide."

☙ My Son

He did not care; he said he did not care.
There were no wrinkles on his winsome face.
He never rode a horse he had to spare;
With whip and spur he could go any place.

There were no shadows hid behind his eyes
He thought, he never had an afterthought.
He did not know that woods and winds were wise
Enough to sweep away the wars he fought.

He did not know, he really did not know
That there was such a tragic thing as love.
He had never seen a surgeon sew
Up things you would rather not be thinking of.

And yet I love the child. It is my fault
He has such foolish fancies of the earth.
He will be surprised to sit below the salt—
He has such gaudy notions of his worth.

Dromedary

A dromedary does not fear the sand.
A dromedary knows there is an end
Of the dry granulated sun-burdened land.
A dromedary has seen tall palm-trees bend
In a green place where moistened greeneries trace
With grass and fern on the long desert's face.

A dromedary understands the dry
Fierce heat of the uncompromising floor
That crumbles, asks of each foot where and why.
A dromedary knows there is a door.
Caravan and caravan go on
Through the dry night to be near green at dawn.

Good Night

Moonlight
Is hidden from my view.
Good night
And none to say it to.

And yet I say *good night, good night,*
Though none are near me that can care.
I say, to save myself from fright,
Good night, good night to the dark air.

ᴄ Elegy V

I do not laugh at all of the nice things:
At the bronze coffin, the gathered flowers,
Nor at the way the lurid contralto sings,
Not at you and the rest of your wasted hours.

This was a nice funeral, my wife was sad;
My children wept their eyes out and the preacher
Said a mouthful. "It was too bad,"
(As she put her arm around my child) said the teacher.

The Legion did its bit and shot a volley
After the ritual at my grave.
My wife seemed to enjoy their noisy folly;
They gave her the empty shells to save.

They have been praised for sins that they committed,
Sanctified for miracles that were tricks,
For virtues they admitted
Unruly lamps with smoky wicks.

A saint is a disorderly sort of person,
Half mad, insanely right,
To whom reason is an unholy perversion—
His night is a ghastly revealing light.

He remembers strange corners in his dreams.
Once he is awake he sets out to find them.
He is more crafty and cunning than he seems.
He has smelled the secrets, has teeth to unwind them.

The sweat of his labor is as sweet as love.
God watches him in his soporific charity
And half regrets all the answers of
His ferment from reasonable intelligence and clarity.

❧ A Skull

The water moves easily now through your great eyes,
Now your eyes are not there, that stopped so many tears,
That were so azure and so dubiously wise
They stopped the liquid of so many years.

Now that your skull is emptied out of brain
All the misgivings that you had are gone;
All the gray entrails made to measure pain
Will not be there to wonder at the dawn.

Now that your wisdom is dispensed of bone
I see the washed-out skull that held your knowledge.
How did you dare to stand up all alone
Brave with the little learning of your college?

Sonnet

My love is all there is. It is enough.
I found a face in all the million faces,
Dark eyes that every other hue erases.
Pink cloud and sky-blue blossoms all afluff
Are airy nonsense, insubstantial stuff,
Now I have brought to earth your airy graces
And put your wondering in my leathery traces—
Here, you are ironing out my linen cuff.

There, you were ailing with the child we had
And the anonymous growth grew to be a man.
For all your pain you forgave and were glad:
I must have a daughter—so your thought ran.
My love is all there is: the children came,
I am still in love—but wasn't it a game?

Many Loves in One

I have not had many loves but one:
One wife can be a harem to the soul;
One pair of eyes reflect enough of sun
So a strumpet would seem a tong-carried coal.

I have had many loves in one,
A beauty with giggling eyes,
Then after twenty years were run
A gravity, spun with beauty, wise.

O child of my most secret heart,
You will never, never know my love;
So clumsy is my only art
You will not know what I am thinking of.

It seems a pity—a pity to me
For I feel your love whenever you look,
Whenever I look I read you through
As a man does when he reads a favorite book.

There are a thousand prayers to pray,
At least a hundred discordant bells,
As many priests as beggars to pay
For passports out of confusing hells.

The cow in her third belly melts the lawn,
The golden maple sheds her wilting leaves,
The oak has fallen and is quarter sawn,
And close-cropped grain slouches in mouldering sheaves.

The shiny world will soon be put away,
Roses in memory and wheat in bins,
White clouds in little brains, to stay;
The slag of iron mines rolled into pins—

There is no passport for a giddy dawn;
There is no rest for a resplendent moon.
Only white paper that we write upon
Keeps us from forgetting them too soon.

The Flaw

Good morning to another day.
Yesterday is so far away,
Where I walked and what I did
Were slammed underneath a lid.

Whom I loved and what I said
Has gone with silence off to bed;
What I read and what I thought
Is with slumber overwrought.

But oh there is some awful flaw!
I half remember what I saw.

Poem in a Dark Room

The toe that burst the lily pod
With a gentle shoe was shod.
Ask of darkness, ask of dawn
Whence he came, where he has gone.

With lugubrious surmise,
Rhythm on her stealthy tread
May by stratagem surprise
The vague encampment of the dead.

Be Mannerly

You must be mannerly with death.
A sudden heart attack, a pang,
A sudden failure of your breath
And you have done it with a bang.

A leaky vein may cut off half
The limbs and speech that once were yours,
So you can never walk nor laugh,
And doctors are at a loss for cures.

It does not do you any good;
It does no good to any one.
You are not better for your food.
You are not better for the sun.

Be mannerly, I say, with death,
Mother—you were born to die.
No prophet had a "sooth" or "saith"
Except one ending in a sigh.

Christ in the Blessed Sacrament

I gave this one my flesh,
That one my blood.
I had them unmesh
As much as they could.
They said: "Put them together,
The pea and the pod.
Let us see whether
They are equal to God."
Then they had scrapple,
God's Son for a feast.
They built them a chapel
And hired them a priest.
But oh how I fooled them!
He that took wine,
The wine overruled him:
Swore the bread was not mine.
And he that had bread
Distrusted the wine.
I laughed and I fled,
Disputed, divine.

O God, Be Cautious

I must build an altar, light a fire,
Carve or cast gods, and adore them.
Pour holy water on desire.
Golden calves have seen strange men before them.

Gods should be wary of recruits
—It is dangerous to be a worshiped thing—
Some sullen as mutes, some blind as newts.
You can misjudge them even as they sing.

So many doubtful saints are canonized.
Do not depend too much upon their virtue.
Litanies can be memorized or improvised.
The triviality of prayer can hurt you.

He Built the Reef

Furrows of planets are to Him
No more than turnip-rows are to you.
They roll like billiards at His whim
Whenever He wants to improve His view.

You see Him in a long white beard—
Every sort of lechery is His device.
Every monster and viper that you feared
He thought of twice.

Your virtue is His pleasantry.
Part of His plan is your grief.
He is amused with oxen and peasantry.
He teases the wave. He built the reef.

For This?

Was it for this you took my hand,
To show me all the hollow sky,
To walk me over the dark land,
To hear the withered sedges sigh?
Was it for this you spilled my beer,
And let the door behind me bang?
Tell me what is it that you hear,
What lark, what linnet was it sang?